Freda Haslam

SALZBURG
IN
PICTURE

The History

c. 40/50 A. D.: The Roman settlement of Juvavum is raised to the status of a municipality by Emperor Claudius (41 – 54 A. D.).

c. 480: The Romans abandon the city of Juvavum, which falls into decay.

c. 700: The Franconian Bishop Rupert is instructed by the Bavarian Duke Theodo to set up a bishopric at the ruined Juvavum. He founds St. Peter's Abbey and Nonnberg Priory.

774: Bishop Virgil (745 – 784), an Irishman by birth, completes the first cathedral church.

798: Arno, a distinguished scholar and founder of the Salzburg library, is created Archbishop and Metropolitan of Bavaria at the instigation of Charlemagne.

10th century: The archbishops of Salzburg become feudal princes of the German Empire.

991 – 1023: Archbishop Hartwik enlarges Virgil's cathedral. Beginnings of a secular township, at first unfortified, which serves as place of transshipment on the trade route between Italy and Germany.

1060 – 1088: Archbishop Gebhard supports Pope Gregory VII in his quarrel with Emperor Henry IV. Construction work is begun on the Hohensalzburg Fortress.

1106 – 1147: Being a supporter of the Pope, Archbishop Konrad I is one of the most important personalities in the German episcopacy. A new bishop's court is built and the Fortress is enlarged. The Augustinian Rule is adopted by the Cathedral Chapter.

1167: Supporters of the Emperor Frederick Barbarossa burn down the town including all its churches.

1177 – 1183: Archbishop Konrad III of Wittelsbach, the first cardinal of the archdiocese, becomes "Legatus Natus". The Emperor and the Pope conclude a peace treaty and the town is rebuilt. The Romanesque minster is built.

1200 – 1246: Archbishop Eberhard II of Regensburg.

End of 13th century: Closer contacts with Austria.

1365 – 1396: The archdiocese expands to reach its greatest extent. The secular part of the city grows.

15 th century: Important buildings are constructed in the secular part of the city and the burghers strive for their own city administration.

1478: In the quarrel between Archbishop Bernard von Rohr and Emperor Frederick II the townspeople side with the Emperor and are rewarded with privileges.

1495 – 1519: Archbishop Leonhard von Keutschach forces the townspeople to renounce their privileges and puts an end to their struggle for the rights of a free imperial city, thus opening the way for the subsequent autocratic building programmes. The court life is marked by great splendour. Extensions are made to the Fortress. Expulsion of the Jews.

1519 – 1540: Archbishop Cardinal Lang von Wellenburg. Secularisation of the Cathedral Chapter. Released from the Rule, the canons form the city's aristocracy. Upheavals of the Reformation. Rebellious peasants unsuccessfully besiege the Fortress.

1541: Theophrastus Bombastus von Hohenheim, known as Paracelsus, dies in Salzburg.

1587 – 1612: Archbishop Wolf Dietrich von Raitenau, great-nephew of the Medici Pope Pius IV, turns medieval Salzburg into a baroque metropolis. He has the burnt-out cathedral and 55 large houses torn down and, working according to plans by Vincenzo Scamozzi, creates the four great squares, thus determining the present lay-out of the city. He is captured during a quarrel with Duke Maximilian of Bavaria and held prisoner in the Fortress until his death.

1612 – 1619: Archbishop Markus Sittikus, Count of Hohenems, continues the vigorous building activities of his cousin Wolf Dietrich, which showed considerable influence from Italy. Construction of the Cathedral and Hellbrunn Palace by Santino Solari. First performance of an opera north of the Alps.

1619 – 1653: Archbishop Paris, Count of Lodron. Consecration of the Cathedral (1628). Successful policy of neutrality in the Thirty Years' War. Extensions to the Fortress and construction of the northern bastions. The University is founded (1622).

Archbishop Marcus Sitticus with a painting by Arsenio Mascagni showing Hellbrunn under construction

1687 – 1709: Archbishop Ernst Johann, Count of Thun. Johann Bernhard Fischer von Erlach builds the great baroque churches and Klesheim Palace.

1709 – 1727: Archbishop Franz Anton, Prince of Harrach. Extensions to the Mirabell Palace and to the Residence by Lukas von Hildebrandt.

1727 – 1744: Archbishop Leopold Anton Eleutherius, Lord Firmian. Expulsion of 20,000 Protestant mountain peasants. Schloss Leopoldskron built.

1753 – 1771: Archbishop Siegmund III, Count von Schrattenbach, patron of Wolfgang Amadeus Mozart. It was he who made the family's journeys abroad possible.

1756: Wolfgang Amadeus Mozart is born in Salzburg.

1772 – 1803: Hieronymus, Count von Colloredo quarrels and eventually breaks with Mozart. A rationalist by temperament, he helps to introduce the Enlightenment to Salzburg. Founding of important periodicals.

1803: Secularisation of the ecclesiastical principality, which is granted to the Emperor's brother, Archduke Ferdinand, as compensation for having been expelled from Tuscany.

1810 – 1816: Salzburg is ceded to Bavaria. Loss of the court, dissolution of the University and the end of economic independence.

1816: Salzburg is finally incorporated into Austria.

1818: A great fire destroys parts of the city on the right bank of the Salzach.

1st half of the 19th century: Salzburg, reduced to political insignificance and with the grass growing in its squares, is discovered by painters of the Romantic age.

1850: Salzburg becomes an independent crown province of the Austrian Empire.

2nd half of the 19th century: Senseless demolition of the Lodron fortifications, which only comes to an end after the Linz Gate has been pulled down.

1917: Foundation of the Salzburg Festival Association.

1924 – 1938: Construction of the first Festival Hall (Eduard Hütter, Clemens Holzmeister). Hofmannsthal's conception of the "City as a stage setting" is realized.

1938: German troops enter the city, which becomes the capital of the Province of Salzburg in the Eastern March of the Third Reich.

1944 – 1945: Bomb damage to the Cathedral, in the Embankment District, to Mozart's house and in many other places.

1945: Entry of American troops, who occupy the city until 1955. Salzburg becomes the capital of the Austrian federal province bearing the same name.

From 1950: Considerable expansion of the city.

1962: Reconstitution of the University.

The Fortress

Again and again the visitor's gaze is drawn back to the fortress of Hohensalzburg. Now more than nine centuries old, it is one of the city's great landmarks. Construction work on it began in the 11th century and was completed in 1681. Right down the centuries, Hohensalzburg has always remained unconquered, proving impregnable for enemy troops.

View of the City of Salzburg, with Untersberg in the background

By rack-and-pinion railway to the fortress

Oriel in the inner courtyard of the fortress

The fortress of Hohensalzburg towers 120 metres above the city. Leonhard von Keutschach, who resided here from 1495 to 1519, was responsible for giving it the imposing form we see today. His distinctive coat of arms is to be found all over the castle, a reminder of the outstanding role he played in its construction. Extending over an area of 30,000 sqm, the fortress is the largest preserved castle in Central Europe. After 1800, it was used as military barracks, as a military detention centre, and as a store. Today it is one of Austria's most popular museums and is "conquered", in a peaceful sense, by over a million visitors each year. In the courtyard of the castle, Leonhard

Footpath up to the fortress

von Keutschach erected a memorial to himself: in a niche on the outside wall of St. George's, a late-Gothic church, there is a marble relief that shows the prelate, dressed in his vestments, raising his hand in blessing. St. George's was built in 1502; its inside walls are decorated with reliefs of Christ and the twelve apostles, masterpieces carved out of red marble.

The church in the fortress, built by Archbishop Leonhard and dedicated by him to St. George

On St. George's Day – April 23 – every year, Salzburg's militia, dressed in their traditional costumes, hold a service of commemoration in St. George's Church.

The fortress, which looks so forbidding from the outside, contains some very special gems, the princes' apartments. Whereas the walls and ceiling of the "Golden Hall" are strewn with gilded knobs, the "Golden Chamber" contains Austria's most beautiful late-Gothic tiled stove. This masterpiece was constructed by a stove-fitter from Salzburg in 1501.

Late-Gothic tiled stove in Hohensalzburg's "Golden Chamber"

The City

"Salzburg is like a beautiful dream that one constantly longs to keep hold of so that it won't slip away like a charming yet fleeting fairy-tale" – this is how the poet Nikolaus Lenau dreamt of Salzburg, a city whose praises have been sung many times. Painted by artists and praised by poets – this is how Salzburg has become world-famous.

**View of the city
from Hohensalzburg**

Round the Cathedral: souvenir shops, horse-drawn carriages and lots of visitors

One of Salzburg's outstanding features is the Cathedral, the largest of the city's 36 churches. It can accommodate more than 10,000 worshippers. The first cathedral was built on this site by Archbishop Virgil from 767–774. At the end of the 12th century, it was replaced by a five-aisled basilica, which was gutted by fire in 1598. The third cathedral, the present-day building, was badly damaged by bombs in 1944, during the Second World War, but was lovingly restored to its former splendour after the war had ended. The font came from the old cathedral: it is the font at which – according to the chronicles – Wolfgang Amadeus Mozart was solemnly baptised.

Salzburg Cathedral

The Carabinieri Hall in the Residence Palace

Altogether seven archbishops were involved in the building of Salzburg's Residence Palace – what had been begun by Wolf Dietrich was completed by the city's last great architect, Anton, Prince Harrach, in 1710. Today grand events still take place in the Palace's magnificent halls.

The carillon

The carillon rings out from its tower three times a day: at 7 a.m., 11 a.m., and at 6 p.m., 35 hammers strike 35 bells.

The view from Residenzplatz towards the University Church and, further up the hillside, the Grand Café Winkler and the Casino.

Each morning, University Square is the setting for a market at which fresh fruit and vegetables, eggs and butter are offered for sale in noisy but charming fashion.

A typical feature of the city are the houses with courtyards through which one can take a short cut from one street in the city centre to the next. These courtyards count among the most delightful characteristics of the city, and they are always good for a surprise: sometimes one may contain a secluded inn garden that invites the visitor to tarry a while, another time there is a confectioner's shop, while occasionally the irresistible aroma of spice cakes wafts out of one of the countless shops that make the courtyards so fascinating. Many of them deck themselves out in their Sunday best, too: in summer, their walls are a mass of flowers and luxuriant greenery.

University Square

An inner courtyard
with colourful
window-boxes and
a stall selling
spice bouquets

Eating out in Salzburg

This dessert, which goes by the name of "Salzburger Nockerl", is ordered probably more often than any other sweet dish in Salzburg. Strictly speaking, the main ingredient in "Nockerl" is – air! But what develops around the air is described by connoisseurs as being "simply heavenly"!

No path to Salzburg fails to lead the visitor to the street called Getreidegasse where Mozart's Birthplace is to be found, a house that has become a place of pilgrimage for millions of people from all over the world. The street is, however, interesting in its own right, too, because of its shops; and it is really worth seeing, above all, for the numerous mediaeval shops signs that recall the old trades and crafts once practised here.

Getreidegasse

Mozart's Birthplace

The house where Wolfgang Amadeus Mozart was born in 1756 is now the property of the Mozarteum, an international foundation. A museum today, the house is the most important memorial to the great composer in Salzburg. It contains, among other mementoes, Mozart's piano, the violin he played as a child, and the clavichord on which he composed "Titus", "The Magic Flute" and his "Requiem".

The Salzburg Festival

The Salzburg Festival, one of the greatest events in the theatrical world, was started in 1920 by Hugo von Hofmannsthal, Max Reinhardt and Richard Strauss. And, right up to the present day, seven decades later, directors, actors, conductors and singers regard it as a special honour to be invited to appear before the thousands of art-lovers who flock here every year.

Collegiate Church

The splendid Collegiate Church, also called the University Church, was built by Fischer von Erlach in Baroque style.

From an architectural point of view, the Franciscan Church is one of Salzburg's most varied and interesting churches.

Franciscan Church

St. Peter's Graveyard

St. Peter's Abbey

When somebody talks about St. Peter's, he means the graveyard, the church and the abbey as well. It was here, on sacred soil, that Salzburg's long history began, after the stormy period of the Great Migrations. This place is the cradle of the ecclesiastical principality. The oldest church, which was built by Salzburg's founder, St. Rupert, in about 696, stood on the site of the present-day Holy Cross Chapel, directly beside the interesting communal crypt.

Horses – horses – horses: although the automobile has already conquered the whole world, it is almost impossible to imagine Salzburg without "one horse-power" as a unit of measurement. Beside the Horse Pond, a fountain in Sigmundplatz, explorers of Salzburg will find themselves surrounded by horses made of flesh and blood. And there are a fair number of bridal couples who even have themselves driven to the Registry Office by "two horse-power", in a horse-drawn carriage.

The almost 300-year-old Horse Pond in Sigmundplatz, with a statue of a horse-tamer in the centre of it

On hot days in summer, the Chapter Horse Pond in the elegant Kapitelplatz (Chapter Square) is like a magnet for visitors to the city on the River Salzach. Clear water from mountain streams splashes constantly down over the stone steps. In the middle of the fountain stands the massive figure of Neptune, carved in stone. In one hand he holds his trident, with the other he caresses the mane of a magnificent creature, half-horse, half-fish.

Many of Salzburg's fountains are outstanding examples of the sculptor's art. And, again and again, the observer comes across horses hewn in stone. In the Residence Fountain, the horses have been spouting water towards the heavens for centuries.

Salzburg's Residence Fountain   The Chapter Horse Pond

**Kapitelplatz –
view of the
Cathedral from
the fountain**

Antretter House in Mozartplatz, with its 18th-cent. Rococo facade

Salzburg is truly a place worth visiting, and everyone wandering through the city on foot will be captivated by the inimitable atmosphere to be found in its ancient and idyllic streets. Every guest is invited to take a part in the play that is constantly being performed here.

Each courtyard in Salzburg looks different, and every single one is an architectural jewel.

Salzburg has close on four hundred streets, alleys and squares. Not until 1800 did the French authorities number the houses in order to make it easier to find billets for their soldiers. It's most fun to go shopping early in the morning, when it's possible to stroll in leisurely fashion through the tranquil streets before the great mass of tourists arrives. The city has, by the way, developed into one of Europe's major centres of high fashion in the last twenty years. The shops selling Salzburg's typical and traditional Austrian clothing have been joined by boutiques whose wares come from the great, wide world of fashion, ranging from Armani to Yves Saint-Laurent. Apart from its fashion shops, Salzburg is also renowned as a city of antique-dealers and jewellers. It is one of those places where select shopping facilities are to be found right beside exquisite cultural amenities.

Shopping in quaint old shops that offer goods which are in the forefront of international fashion as well as reflecting a sense of tradition

The city as a stage-set

Salzburg is not just the venue for huge open-air concerts featuring famous singers like Stevie Wonder and Tina Turner; the city on the Salzach also provides the background for events that foster the local traditions of this region. Salzburg is frequently a meeting-place for groups showing their affinity with earlier generations in their costumes, their dances and their festivities. For example, Corpus Christi, one of the most important festivals in the Catholic Church's calendar, is celebrated in style in Salzburg Cathedral.

Once a year, Salzburg's Residenzplatz, flanked by the venerable Residence Palace, the Cathedral and the tower with the carillon in it, is the scene of a fair held in honour of St. Rupert, the founder of the city and the patron saint

St. Rupert's Fair, held to commemorate the missionary who founded Salzburg about 700 A. D.

of the Federal Province of Salzburg. With its big wheel and merry-go-rounds, it is a popular attraction for young and old. Anyone visiting Salzburg around September 24 can enjoy all the fun of St. Rupert's Fair along with the local residents.

A fair is also a welcome opportunity to revive traditional dances. In the picture above right, Salzburg's "Bandltanz" can be seen, a dance with ribbons that is performed beneath the linden tree in the castle courtyard at Hohensalzburg during St. George's Fair. At St. Rupert's Fair, a dance called the "Altsalzburger Bindertanz" is always performed.

**The "Altsalzburger Bindertanz"
against the background
of the Residence Palace**

A special feature of Salzburg in the weeks before Christmas is the fair known as the "Christkindlmarkt", which is held in the square that is always the setting for "Everyman", the world-famous play performed at the Salzburg Festival each year. Against the impressive backdrop of Salzburg Cathedral and right beside the Franciscan Church, the Christmas market is attractive not only for shoppers but also for admirers of the beautiful architecture surrounding the stalls.

Tiny shops in picturesque courtyards

Christmas decorations in Getreidegasse

Narrow courtyards with secluded corners, brightly illuminated shop windows, concealed arcades with barrel vaults, a bakery with enticing smells coming from it – that is Salzburg during Advent. In this "most peaceful season of the year", the city exudes that charm for which it is famous; and, even on rather hectic shopping days, the streets and squares manage to preserve their romantic atmosphere.

Invitation to a Christmas shopping expedition

Mirabell Palace, the grand staircase

One of Salzburg's most beautiful staircases is in the Mirabell Palace. It leads up to the Marble Hall, where civil marriages are conducted. All the way up the stairs, there is an intricately interwoven balustrade with cheerful little Baroque cherubs on it, modelled by Ralph Donner. It cannot be sheer coincidence that engaged couples from all over the world choose to get married in these magnificent surroundings.

One reason for the palace's popularity is the tragic story of the love-affair between Wolf Dietrich, the Roman Catholic Archbishop of Salzburg, and Salome Alt, the beautiful daughter of a prominent citizen. She bore him 15 children. Wolf Dietrich had the original part of the palace built as a visible expression of his love for Salome. Life in the palace is reputed to have had a fairy-tale quality about it, but it was a fairy tale that was to end abruptly and tragically.

**overleaf:
View of Hohensalzburg
from the Mirabell Gardens**

Cultural Life

Salzburg is an important centre in the world of music, but this is not really surprising, considering that Mozart was born here in 1756, that Michael Haydn came to work in Salzburg and remained here until his death in 1806, and that Carl Maria von Weber, who was taught counterpoint by Michael Haydn, lived here from 1797 until 1802. Unanimous in their veneration for Mozart are the thousands and thousands of music-lovers who each year follow the trail of the *genius loci* in the house in Getreidegasse where the great composer was born, and in the house in Makartplatz where he lived.

The opening ceremony of the Festival

A traditional event in Salzburg on the evening the Festival opens is the ceremonial firing of salvos by the "Prangstutzenschützen" in their splendid uniforms.

The "Drama of the Life and Death of the Rich Man, Everyman", performed in front of the Cathedral during the Festival, is attended by lovers of the theatre from more than 70 nations. It has always been possible to find famous actors and actresses who regard it as an honour to take on one of the leading roles in this morality play.

Everyman

Salzburg's Festival Theatre Building

The two festival theatres in Salzburg, the Small Festival Theatre and the Great Festival Theatre, were both designed by the Austrian architect Clemens Holzmeister. Including the former riding school, which is built into the cliffs and which also forms part of the theatre complex, the three auditoria have a seating capacity of about 5000 in all.

The festival theatres have long been a byword for brilliant artistic productions.

Among the popular events that take place on the eve of the Festival is the "Old Salzburg Torchlight Dance", which is always performed beside the Residence Fountain after darkness has fallen.

previous page:
Performance of Beethoven's "Fidelio"
in the Great Festival Theatre

Musical theatre and poetry,
concerts and recitals,
mime and dance –
at many different venues in
and near the city –
a city of culture

Wolfgang Amadeus Mozart was born during a restless but dramatic epoch, and died before reaching his 36th birthday. His father, Leopold Mozart, moved from Augsburg to Salzburg, where he had a post as violinist in the Archbishop's Cathedral Orchestra. His wife, Maria Anna Pertl, who came from St. Gilgen in the Salzkammergut, gave birth to seven children, only two of whom survived – Wolfgang Amadeus and Maria Anna, known as Nannerl. Johann Nepomuk della Croce, a painter from Salzburg, recorded a family scene for posterity: the young Mozart and his sister Nannerl are playing the piano four-handed, Leopold Mozart is to be seen leaning on the piano, while the whole scene is dominated by a portrait of Mozart's mother, Maria Anna, who had died some time previously.

overleaf:
Concert in Salzburg's
Mozarteum

The Mozart Family

Salzburg Marionette Theatre

Chamber music in the fortress of Hohensalzburg

**Salzburg's State Theatre,
a late 19th-century building**

**Musicians from South America
beside Mozart's statue**

The Salzburg Advent Concerts, which appeal to so many people because they create just the right mood for the approaching Christmas season, have counted among the major annual events in Salzburg since 1946. More than a million people have attended these concerts, which were initiated by Tobias Reiser. The stage of the Great Festival Theatre is the setting for an exquisite presentation of Salzburg's folk-music and folk-culture by men, women and children from the city.

Every year the audience is enchanted by the beautiful Advent music

The nativity play, an especially popular feature

Folk-music played on typical instruments like the zither, the harp, the dulcimer and the double-bass – the Advent Concert, an occasion unique in Austria

Michael Pacher's Madonna

A particularly precious work of art is the Gothic madonna carved in wood by Michael Pacher in 1498. It is to be found in Salzburg's Franciscan Church.

The tiny Grillinger Altar, named after the man who donated it, a priest from Lungau, is the work of an unknown goldsmith from Salzburg. It still stands in St. Mary's Parish Church (Mariapfarr).

The Grillinger Altar

As Christmas approaches, crib scenes are set up in many churches and farmhouses in the Salzburg region: carved figures of Joseph and Mary, the Christ Child and the Three Kings recall the story of Christ's nativity. Probably the best-known maker of such cribs in recent decades was Xandl Schläffer from Saalfelden, who constructed more than 800 of them.

A Salzburg crib scene

Nature and architecture: creation and creativity in harmony

Stone-carved unicorn in the Mirabell Gardens

Salzburg is a real eldorado for photographers and painters. Unusual motifs present themselves at every turn: here, for instance, is a view of Hohensalzburg Fortress taken from the Mirabell Gardens, with a stone-carved unicorn in the foreground.

**overleaf:
A spice bouquet,
a souvenir from Salzburg**

House of Nature (Haus der Natur)

Probably nowhere else in the world is there anything resembling Salzburg's "House of Nature" (Haus der Natur). In it, living things ally themselves with lifeless objects on an adventurous expedition through the world of nature. United here under one roof, the observer can find what is usually spread out over the whole globe – from the exciting, colourful world beneath the sea to true-to-life reconstructions of the habitats of crocodiles, snakes and exotic lizards.

The "Portrait of a Girl" is one of the main works painted by Oskar Kokoschka during his early Expressionist phase. It was painted about 1913 and now hangs in the Rupertinum, the gallery of modern art.

**Oskar Kokoschka,
"Portrait of a Girl"**

Salzburg's Carolino-Augusteum Museum was founded in 1843. Destroyed during the Second World War, it reopened in 1966. Its collection includes, for example, Carl Spitzweg's "Promenade" and some works by Hans Markart, a native of Salzburg who is associated with a group of Viennese artists. This portrait of Baroness Waldberg, another of the museum's exhibits, was also painted by Makart.

**Hans Makart,
"Baroness Waldberg"**

F. G. Waldmüller, the leading exponent of Realism in the German-speaking area in the 19th century, painted this landscape in 1834. The picture was donated to the Carolino-Augusteum Museum by the Max Kade Foundation, New York.

**Ferdinand Georg
Waldmüller,
"View of Hallstatt"**

Peter Paul Rubens, "Satyr and Girl with a Basket of Fruit"

One of the paintings in Salzburg's Residence Art Gallery is this picture, entitled "Satyr and Girl with a Basket of Fruit". It was painted by Peter Paul Rubens.

Rubens, the Flemish Baroque painter, worked first of all in Antwerp, before going to Italy in 1600 and then, in 1609, becoming court painter to the Governor of Antwerp. Titian was a major influence on his work. His "Allegorical Portrait of Charles V as the Ruler of the World" was purchased for the Residence Art Gallery from Great Britain in 1966.

Peter Paul Rubens, "Allegorical Portrait of Charles V as the Ruler of the World"

The famous fountains in Hellbrunn

To the great delight of the people of Salzburg and of their summer visitors, open-air festivals have been held at Hellbrunn again in recent years. On two weekends in August, the palace grounds form the setting for a feast of music, dancing and singing. As in the days of Marcus Sitticus, everyone is invited to come along and enjoy themselves. And, when Hellbrunn laughs, this palace, which was originally intended as a place of pleasure, is like a graceful primadonna using her seductive charm to win her audience's approval.

Theatre against an impressive background – Hellbrunn Palace ...

Fountains everywhere – their water an element full of bubbling joie de vivre

The entrance to Neptune's Cave

... or in the open air in the leafy park

Around Salzburg

Anif Castle is first mentioned in documents dating from about 1550. It had an eventful history before Count Arco-Stepperg had it almost completely rebuilt in neo-Gothic style between 1838 and 1848 according to designs of his own. He had gathered the ideas for these designs while travelling in France and England. The result is a building with geometrically arranged windows and towers, with oriels and balconies, and with a terrace surrounded by a crenellated balustrade.

Anif Castle   **Lake Matt (Mattsee)**

Maria Plain

This beautiful pilgrimage church is in North-East Salzburg. Archbishop Max Gandolph had it built between 1671 and 1674 on the site of a wooden chapel that had been erected in 1652 to house a miracle-working portrait of the Madonna.

Leopoldskron Palace

Leopoldskron Palace, surely Salzburg's finest secular building dating from the Baroque period, is closely associated with water, just like the summer residence at Hellbrunn – it stands beside a beautifully designed artificial lake, which was previously the archbishops' private fishpond. The Palace was built in 1736 by a professor of mathematics, Bernard Stuart, who was also a member of the Benedictine order.

Hellbrunn
Summer Palace

Hellbrunn, dating from the early Baroque period, is the acme of pleasure, gaiety and playful coquetry. Among the sights in this fascinating garden of wonders built by Marcus Sitticus, the nephew and successor of Wolf Dietrich, are labyrinthine waterways, mazes, the so-called Playground of the Graces, and a zoo containing exotic animals.

A million visitors come to Hellbrunn every year, partly because of its fountains, which are not only a pleasure to look at, but may also provide an unexpected cooling shower on a hot summer's day: imagine sitting down for a rest on an inviting-looking stone bench and having – quite without warning – a fine but powerful jet of crystal clear water come spurting out of it. Marcus Sitticus is said to have played this joke on his guests whenever the company, drunk with wine, abandoned themselves to noisy merriment. Only one single bench – the Archbishop's – always remained dry, so that the ecclesiastical prince could take full and unimpaired pleasure in the discomfort of the other revellers.

In 1700, Archbishop Johann Ernst, Count Thun, well-known for his enthusiasm for building, commissioned Fischer von Erlach to design a palace to be named "Favorita". An engraving of this projected building of great magnificence is to be found in Fischer's "Proposal for a Historic Piece of Architecture". In fact, what was constructed at Klessheim between 1700 and 1709 is only a tiny part of the ambitious original design. Count Thun's successor, Franz Anton von Harrach, continued the building work, but the palace was not furnished and lived in until after 1732, under Archbishop Leopold Anton Firmian.

Klessheim Palace

Air links with the airports of the world

Salzburg Airport was first opened in 1926. After a somewhat chequered history, the time for its re-integration into the international air network came in 1950. By extending the runway to a length of 2500 m in 1983, the authorities created the preconditions for environmentally friendly jumbo jets to take off and land there.

Two faces of the modern age: a paraglider floating down to the valley from the Gaisberg, Salzburg's "own" mountain. Among the other peaks in the background, the imposing silhouette of Mt. Watzmann can be seen; the ascent to its summit is a challenge for ambitious mountaineers from all over the world.

Paragliding in the Salzburg region

Maria Bühel in Oberndorf

It takes just under half an hour to travel by car from Salzburg to Maria Bühel Church in Oberndorf. A memorial chapel erected in the village in 1937 reminds the visitor that it was here that the celebrated Christmas carol "Silent Night" was composed by Franz Xaver Gruber to words written by Joseph Mohr.

Salzburg is beautiful at all seasons of the year, but it is surely at its most romantic in the winter. Once the bustle of the summer lies buried under a thick white blanket of snow, the visitor can go for long and tranquil walks.

A winter stroll on snowy Mönchsberg

Salzburg may count itself lucky that, in its immediate environment, it has not only scenery of great magnificence, but also numerous facilities for relaxation, sport and leisure activities. In this respect, the Federal Province of Salzburg is a paradise for water-sports enthusiasts, for anglers, for hikers and for lovers of nature.

Peace and quiet for the angler ...

... or for walkers in the extensive forests

The holiday idyll

Every year, the outgoing and friendly people who live here welcome thousands of guests to this popular Austrian holiday region. It is, in particular, the hospitality shown by Salzburg's inhabitants that makes so many people that have visited the area decide to return again – year in, year out.

Sailing on Lake Obertrum

Lake Obertrum in Flachgau near Salzburg is 4.9 sqkm in area. Resorts right on the banks of the lake – Seeham is shown in the photograph – attract thousands of watersports enthusiasts from Austria and from abroad during the summer season.

Refreshing lake air beneath shady trees

And, despite the fact that Salzburg has become a leading tourist centre, its people have not lost their natural quality – they stick faithfully to their customs and traditions. This, in turn, not only contributes to the preservation of local culture but also encourages gregariousness and a spirit of community among the local people.

The starting gun for the big event

Exquisite national costumes – a living tradition

The splendid landscape and mountains of Salzburg

The Federal Province of Salzburg owes its beauty to the fact that it is made up of so many varieties of landscape, from the gentle Alpine foothills to the towering ridges of the Central Alps.

In spite of the tourists who stream through this region in such vast numbers, Salzburg's mountains have remained unharmed and unpolluted. One area where the landscape is particularly delightful is the region on the Salzburg side of the Mitre Mountain (Bischofsmütze).

Salzburg's lakes offer facilities for sport and relaxation

The ancient Samson tradition

"Carrying Samson" is an ancient Lungau custom which is still lovingly observed in the present day. The model for the figure, which weighs 80 kilos and is carried by one single man, is the biblical hero who was so strong that he could rip a lion to pieces. The handsome figure of Samson, clad in a tunic and toga, does not merely stride majestically through the village; should he hear the sound of sweet music, the heavyweight may even risk a little dance!

At the time of the Winter Solstice, young men dress up either as "ugly spirits" (Schiachperchten), or as "beautiful spirits" (Schönperchten) wearing brightly coloured ribbons and sequins.

A terrifying "Schiachperchte"

**The White Horse
Inn on Lake Wolfgang**

Evening on Lake Matt

A trip over the provincial border to Upper Austria: many visitors to Salzburg take the opportunity to travel by excursion steamer from St. Gilgen, which is in the Federal Province of Salzburg, across the lake to St. Wolfgang.

The village with the hotel called The White Horse Inn became world-famous as the setting for Ralph Benatzky's operetta of the same name. In the late-Gothic Church of St. Wolfgang, a place of pilgrimage, there is an ornate high altar by Michael Pacher which is decorated with carved figures and paintings.

Lake Matt is one of the lakes that are especially popular among bathers. The village of Mattsee on its banks goes back to a prehistoric settlement; it has been the site of a monastery since the 8th century.

Published in the
following languages:

German
English
French
Italian
Spanish
Japanese
Czech/Slovak

© **Helmut Schmid Verlag**
Salzburg – Wien – Regensburg

Produktion:
Helmut Schmid Verlag

Text:
Doris Esser

Übersetzung:
Alison M. Thielecke, B. A.

Geschichte:
Verlagsarchiv

Gestaltung:
Fachberatung Peter Stemmle

Reproduktion:
Fuchs Repro, Salzburg

ISBN 3–900284–40–7

Bildnachweis:
Anrather, Fotografie – Cosy-Verlag
Salzburg – Damm, Fotografie –
Fremdenverkehrsbetriebe der Stadt
Salzburg – Haus der Natur – Hotel „Weißes
Rößl" St. Wolfgang – Kirsch, Bildarchiv –
Krieger, Fotografie – Landesverkehrsamt
Salzburg – Marionettentheater Salzburg –
Mozarteum Salzburg – Mozartquartett
Salzburg – Pinzgauer Heimatmuseum
Saalfelden – Schloß Ritzen –
Residenzgalerie Salzburg – Rupertinum
Salzburg – Salzburger Landtourismus –
Salzburger Museum C. A. –
Schmid, Marion.